THE HISTORY OF THE CIVIL RIGHTS MOVEMENT

A History Book for New Readers

Written by
Shadae Mallory, MA

Illustrated by
Angie Alape

ROCKRIDGE PRESS

To my loving parents, John and Ann Marie, who stand by me always. And to Travis, Kristin, and the countless other educators who got me here—from the bottom of my heart: Thank you.

For general information on our other products and services or to obtain technical support, please contact our Customer Care Department within the United States at (866) 744-2665, or outside the United States at (510) 253-0500.

Rockridge Press publishes its books in a variety of electronic and print formats. Some content that appears in print may not be available in electronic books, and vice versa.

Series Designer: Angela Navarra
Interior and Cover Designer: John Calmeyer
Art Producer: Megan Baggott
Editor: Erum Khan
Production Editor: Matthew Burnett
Production Manager: Sandy Noman

Illustrations ©2021 Angie Alape.
National Archives, 51; Pictorial Press Ltd/Alamy, 52; Janine Wiedel Photolibrary/Alamy, 53.
Author photograph courtesy of Cody Devries

Paperback ISBN: 978-1-63807-934-7
Hardcover ISBN: 978-1-63878-613-9
eBook ISBN: 978-1-63807-817-3
R0
Printed in China

CONTENTS

CHAPTER 1
SETTING THE STAGE

Understanding the Civil Rights Movement

The United States of America is home to many different types of people. Not long ago, some of these differences—like skin color—were used to treat people unfairly.

Before the **civil rights** movement, many Black Americans faced **discrimination**. There were laws that said Black people and white people couldn't shop in the same stores or eat at the same restaurants. There were even laws that made Black children go to different schools!

In the 1950s, some heroic people decided it was time to change the laws. They wanted to make America a better place for everyone.

To understand why the civil rights movement happened, we need to look back at how America was formed. The United States used to be part of England. English **colonists** sailed to America in search of a better life. The colonists brought Black people from Africa to work as **enslaved people**. This was how many Black people came to live in the United States.

England did not treat the colonists fairly. In 1776, the colonists wrote the Declaration of Independence. It declared America's freedom from England. It also said that all men were equal—but this wasn't true for enslaved Black people!

Slavery was practiced in the United States from 1619 until the end of the Civil War in 1865.

Even when slavery ended, there was still a LOT to fight for.

You are about to read all about the civil rights movement. You will learn how events in the South affected the entire country. You will meet the leaders who fought for **equality**. Finally, you will see how the **movement** is still inspiring change today!

JUMP –IN THE– THINK TANK

Think about a time when you or someone you know was treated unfairly. How did it make you feel? What are some things you can do to make everyone feel equal?

★ North vs. South ★

After America became independent from England in 1776, it grew. As time passed, Americans began to argue about slavery. By the mid-1800s, many people in the North thought slavery should end. Lots of people in the South disagreed. Southern Americans wanted enslaved people to keep doing the hard work in their fields.

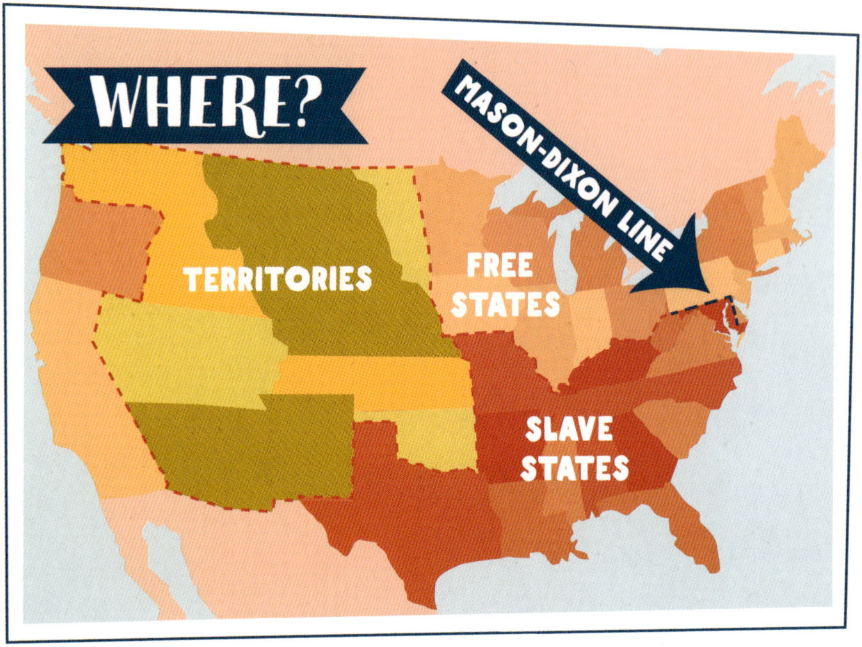

These different views of slavery divided the North and the South. The United States began to seem like two different countries. In 1861, the South tried to make it so. The southern states became their own country—the Confederate States of America. Soon after, the Civil War began. During the Civil War, the South fought to keep slavery, and the North fought to end it.

The North won the Civil War in 1865, and the South rejoined the United States. That same year, the 13th Amendment to the **Constitution of the**

United States made slavery illegal. A few years later, in 1868, the 14th Amendment was passed. It declared that all Black citizens in the United States had the same rights as white citizens.

Sadly, Black people were still not treated fairly after the Civil War. In the 1890s, some states and cities passed **Jim Crow laws** that kept Black and white people separated. These laws made it hard for Black people to go to school, get jobs, or vote in elections.

WHO?

Homer Plessy was a Black shoemaker from Louisiana. He boarded a train in 1892 with a first-class ticket and was arrested for refusing to sit in the train car for Black people at the back of the train.

Some Black people tried to fight Jim Crow. One of them was a man named Homer Plessy, who was arrested for trying to sit in a first-class train car. He took his case all the way to the **Supreme Court**, the highest court in the country. After hearing the *Plessy v. Ferguson* case, the court decided to allow Jim Crow laws, but the states had to make sure the separate schools, stores, and other facilities were equal. These "separate but equal" laws were around for almost 100 years.

WHEN?

1861–1865	DECEMBER 1865	JULY 1868	MAY 1896
The Civil War	The 13th Amendment is added to the Constitution.	The 14th Amendment is added to the Constitution.	*Plessy v. Ferguson* allows Jim Crow laws to stand.

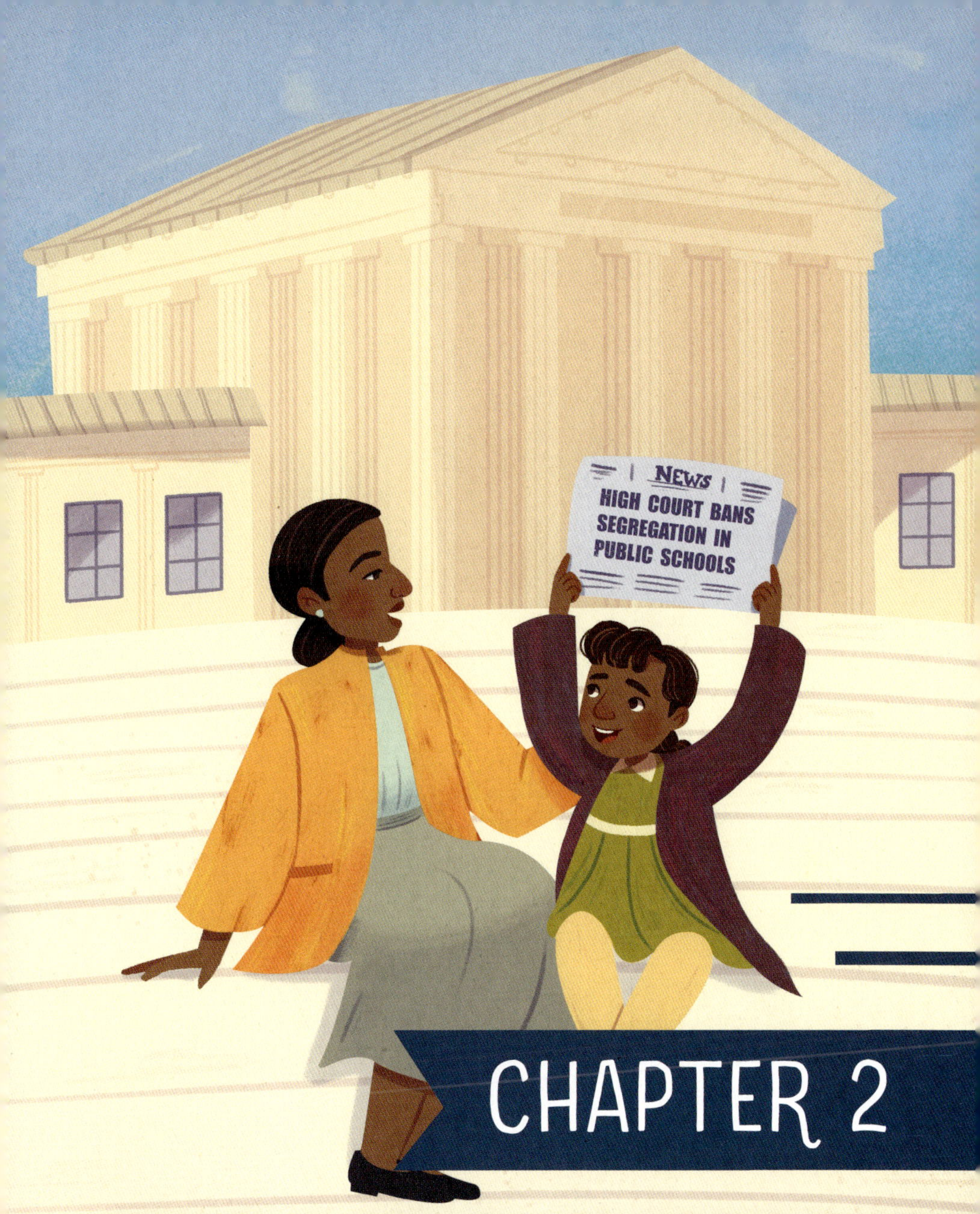

CHAPTER 2

TAKING A STAND

★ Brown v. Board of Education ★

Jim Crow laws made Black children and white children go to **segregated** schools. The schools that Black children went to were very different from the ones white children went to. Many of the schools for Black students were far away from their homes. They were also not as nice as the white schools.

The South had been segregated for more than 80 years when a man named Oliver Brown decided to fight for his daughter Linda. He wanted

her to attend the elementary school near their home in Topeka, Kansas. When the family went to Sumner Elementary School to register Linda, they were turned away because they were Black. Oliver and other parents started talking. They all felt that segregated public schools were unfair.

A group called the **National Association for the Advancement of Colored People (NAACP)** stepped in to help the 13 families in Topeka who wanted to challenge the Board of Education. Other Black families spoke up across the United States. The NAACP was able to make a strong case for the Supreme Court. The NAACP even offered its best lawyer: Thurgood Marshall. Marshall was a Black lawyer who fought for equal rights.

Thurgood Marshall argued that "separate but equal" was actually not equal at all. He convinced the court. In 1954, the Supreme Court voted to end segregation in public schools. The case is now called *Brown v. Board of Education*. It was a very important moment in the fight for civil rights. Even though the Supreme Court voted to end segregation in schools, southern states didn't want to listen. They did everything they could to ignore the decision!

WHO?

Thurgood Marshall was the lawyer for the NAACP who helped win the *Brown v. Board of Education* case. In 1967, Thurgood became the first Black person to be appointed to the Supreme Court. He served his country for 24 years as a Supreme Court justice.

The Montgomery ★ Bus Boycott ★

Jim Crow laws were not just for schools. They were also used to segregate buses and trains. In the South, Black and white people rode in separate parts of public buses. Black people had to sit at the back of the buses, while white people could sit in the front.

In 1955, a brave 15-year-old girl named Claudette Colvin decided not to give her seat on the bus to a white person. She was arrested in Montgomery, Alabama. Claudette's actions inspired others to fight for the freedom to sit where they wanted on public buses. Less than a year later, Rosa Parks followed in Claudette's footsteps and refused to give up her seat, too.

JUMP IN THE THINK TANK

Think of a time when you had to make a hard decision to do the right thing. Was it scary? How did you feel afterward?

Claudette and Rosa believed strongly in their rights. Many civil rights leaders noticed the women's courage. One leader, Dr. Martin Luther King, Jr., wanted to help. Together, civil rights leaders decided to **boycott** (or stop using) the public buses in Montgomery. Dr. King formed the Montgomery Improvement Association (MIA) to help run the bus boycott.

The boycott was originally planned for just December 5, 1955. More than

90 percent of the Black community did not ride the buses that day! Since the boycott was so successful, Black people in Montgomery decided they would not ride the buses until they were **desegregated**. Since many of the people who rode the buses were Black, the bus companies were losing money.

People across the country heard about the Montgomery bus boycott. It inspired some to fight the unfair segregation laws in their own courts. The boycott lasted more than a year. In 1956, the Supreme Court declared that the bus laws in Montgomery were **unconstitutional**.

WHEN?

Brown v Board of Education desegregates schools.

1954

Rosa Parks is arrested.

DECEMBER 1 1955

Montgomery bus boycott occurs in Alabama.

1955–1956

CHAPTER 3

STUDENTS FIGHT BACK

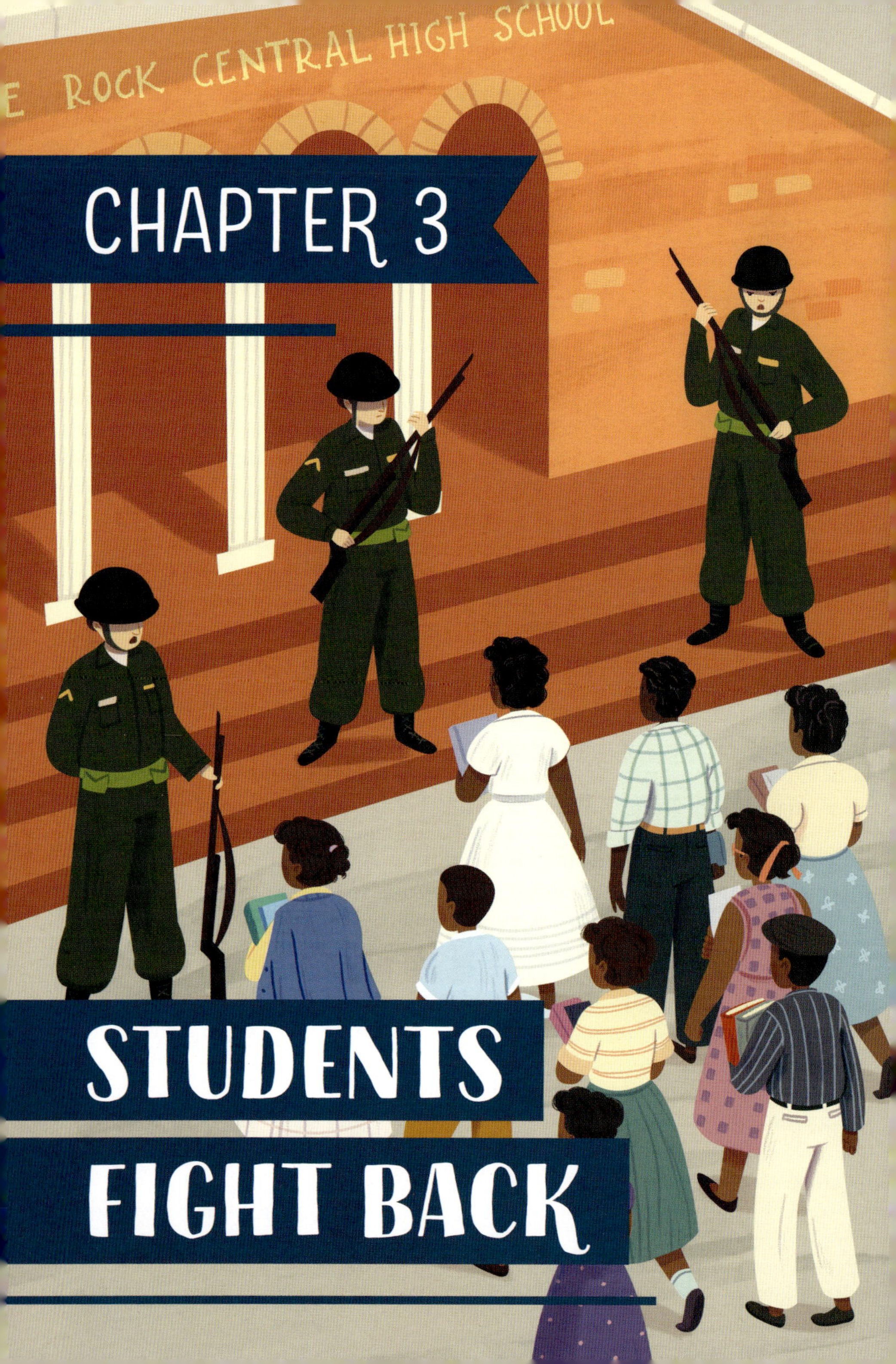

★ New School Rules ★

After *Brown v. Board of Education,* schools in the South still did everything they could to stop Black children from attending. In 1957, nine Black teenagers from Little Rock, Arkansas, were excited for their first day of high school. They had spent their whole lives attending all-Black schools on the far side of town. They couldn't wait to go to a new school with new classmates!

When they arrived at Central High on the first day of school, the Black students were stopped by soldiers with weapons! The governor had sent the **National Guard** to stop them from entering the building. They became known as the Little Rock Nine. They couldn't go to school for three weeks.

On September 25, that changed. President Eisenhower sent US Army soldiers to guard

the students while they attended their classes. Hundreds of white **protestors** called them names and threw things at them. The Little Rock Nine continued to be brave and went to school every day.

WHO?

Ruby Bridges was a young girl who lived in New Orleans, Louisiana. In 1960, Ruby was the first Black student to attend William Frantz Elementary School.

In 1960, another student took a stand in New Orleans, Louisiana. Six-year-old Ruby Bridges was ready to attend William Frantz Elementary. The school made her take a difficult entrance exam, and she passed! Every day, **federal marshals** took her to the school and protected her from protestors. Ruby was the only student in her classroom for the whole year.

Ruby Bridges and the Little Rock Nine were important people in the fight for equal rights. Their bravery and courage helped pave the way for all children to have a better education.

JUMP IN THE THINK TANK

Think about a time when you were courageous. What made you feel that way? How can you help others feel courageous?

Sit-Ins and Freedom Riders

All around the South, Black people found new ways to fight for their civil rights. They chose to use peaceful rather than violent ways to send their message. This is what civil rights leader Dr. Martin Luther King, Jr. preached.

One type of peaceful protest was the **sit-in**. In the 1960s, many stores did not allow Black people to sit at the lunch counters. Four Black

college students wanted to change that rule. They walked into a Woolworth's store in Greensboro, North Carolina, and sat on barstools at the counter.

The white waiter refused to serve them and told them to go to the counter for Black customers instead. The young men didn't move. Angry white customers shouted and pushed them. Some even dumped food and drinks onto the boys! They still did not move from their seats. Their courage inspired others. Sit-ins became a popular way to protest in the South.

Freedom Rides were another kind of peaceful protest. They began in 1961 after the Supreme Court ruled that public transportation between states had to be desegregated. The South strongly disagreed with this decision.

The Freedom Riders started with 13 people: 7 Black people and 6 white people. Together, this brave group rode a Greyhound bus through the South to protest the segregation that was still happening on buses and at bus stations.

The number of Freedom Riders grew. They faced violent attacks, angry mobs, and arrests. Finally, US Attorney General Robert Kennedy

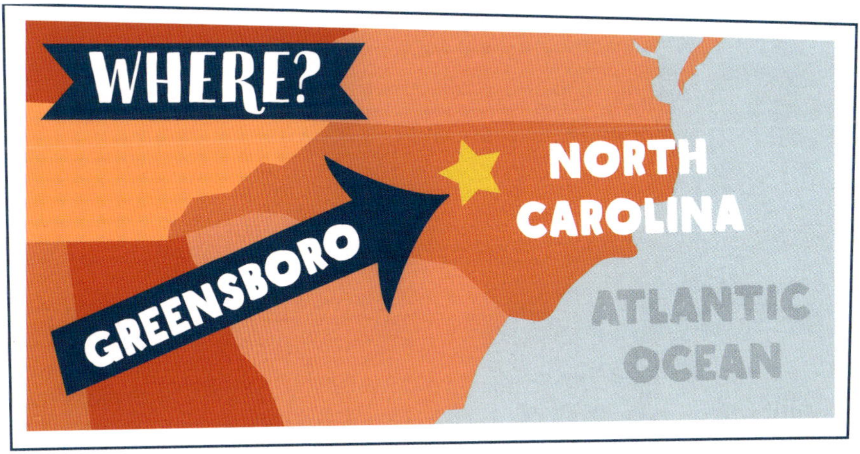

convinced the **Interstate Commerce Commission** to end segregation on their buses and at their bus stations. They did. The Freedom Riders had made a great impact on the civil rights movement.

WHEN?

The Little Rock Nine help desegregate Central High in Little Rock.

1957

First sit-in at Woolworth's in Greensboro.

FEBRUARY 1 1960

Ruby Bridges helps desegregate William Frantz Elementary School.

SEPTEMBER 1960

Freedom Rides begin.

MAY 1961

Interstate Commerce Commission desegregates bus stations.

SEPTEMBER 1961

CHAPTER 4

MARCHING FOR CIVIL RIGHTS

★ Protesting in Birmingham ★

In April 1963, Dr. Martin Luther King, Jr. and the Southern Christian Leadership Conference (SCLC) started a movement to end segregation in Birmingham, Alabama. They asked people to peacefully protest by not shopping at local stores and by having sit-ins and marches. People in Birmingham began to attend Dr. King's meetings. With all the new support,

the SCLC and Dr. King held sit-ins at the library. They also marched to register Black voters at the courthouse!

While the protestors were peaceful, many white people in Birmingham were not. They didn't want to end segregation. They attacked protestors with fire hoses and police dogs. Many protestors, including Dr. King, were arrested! President Kennedy finally sent the National Guard to protect the protestors. By the end of April 1963, many Black adults were tired. They lost hope in their protests. It was around this time that children just like you joined the fight for equality.

JUMP —IN THE— THINK TANK

Imagine you were alive in 1963. How would you feel if you were asked to march for civil rights?

The Children's Crusade started in early May 1963. Thousands of Black children in Birmingham missed school to march for their

rights. They were only kids, but many of them were still arrested by the police! Newspapers across the country and TV news channels showed the children protesting. Many people were inspired by their bravery.

The protests worked. By mid-May, the "White Only" signs were removed from water fountains, lunch counters, and restrooms. There was even a plan to make it possible for Black people to get better jobs. The laws were changing, but Black people still faced discrimination. Dr. King and the other civil rights leaders decided it was time to do something even bigger.

★ The March on Washington ★

After the small successes in Birmingham, Dr. King and the SCLC wanted to lead a giant protest in Washington, DC. Asa Philip Randolph, another civil rights leader, was planning a protest at the same time. Mr. Randolph's group wanted to march to demand higher pay and better treatment of Black workers. Since both men were protesting to help Black Americans, they decided to work together to plan the March on Washington for Jobs and Freedom.

In August 1963, more than 250,000 people met at the Lincoln Memorial. Several civil rights leaders and **activists** spoke at the march, including John Lewis and the NAACP president, Roy Wilkins. After everyone else spoke, Dr. King gave his famous "I Have a Dream" speech. Dr. King wanted everyone to be treated fairly no matter who they were or what

they looked like. It is still one of the most famous speeches in history.

The next year, Congress agreed to write a bill to give Black Americans equal rights. Dr. King and Malcolm X (another brave civil rights leader) each traveled separately to Washington, DC, to help. The bill needed to be edited many times before it was ready for a vote!

Finally, in July 1964, President Lyndon B. Johnson signed the Civil Rights Act. This law officially ended segregation in all public places. The act also made it illegal to discriminate against a person because of their race, color, religion, sex, or **national origin**. It was a very important step for the country to become a welcoming place for *everyone*.

WHO?

Malcolm X was a Black civil rights leader and activist from Omaha, Nebraska. He was a talented minister and fought hard to help create a better future for Black Americans.

WHEN?

The Birmingham Campaign begins.	"White Only" and "Black Only" signs are removed in Birmingham.	The March on Washington for Jobs and Freedom takes place.	The Civil Rights Act is passed.
APRIL 1963	MAY 1963	AUGUST 1963	JULY 1964

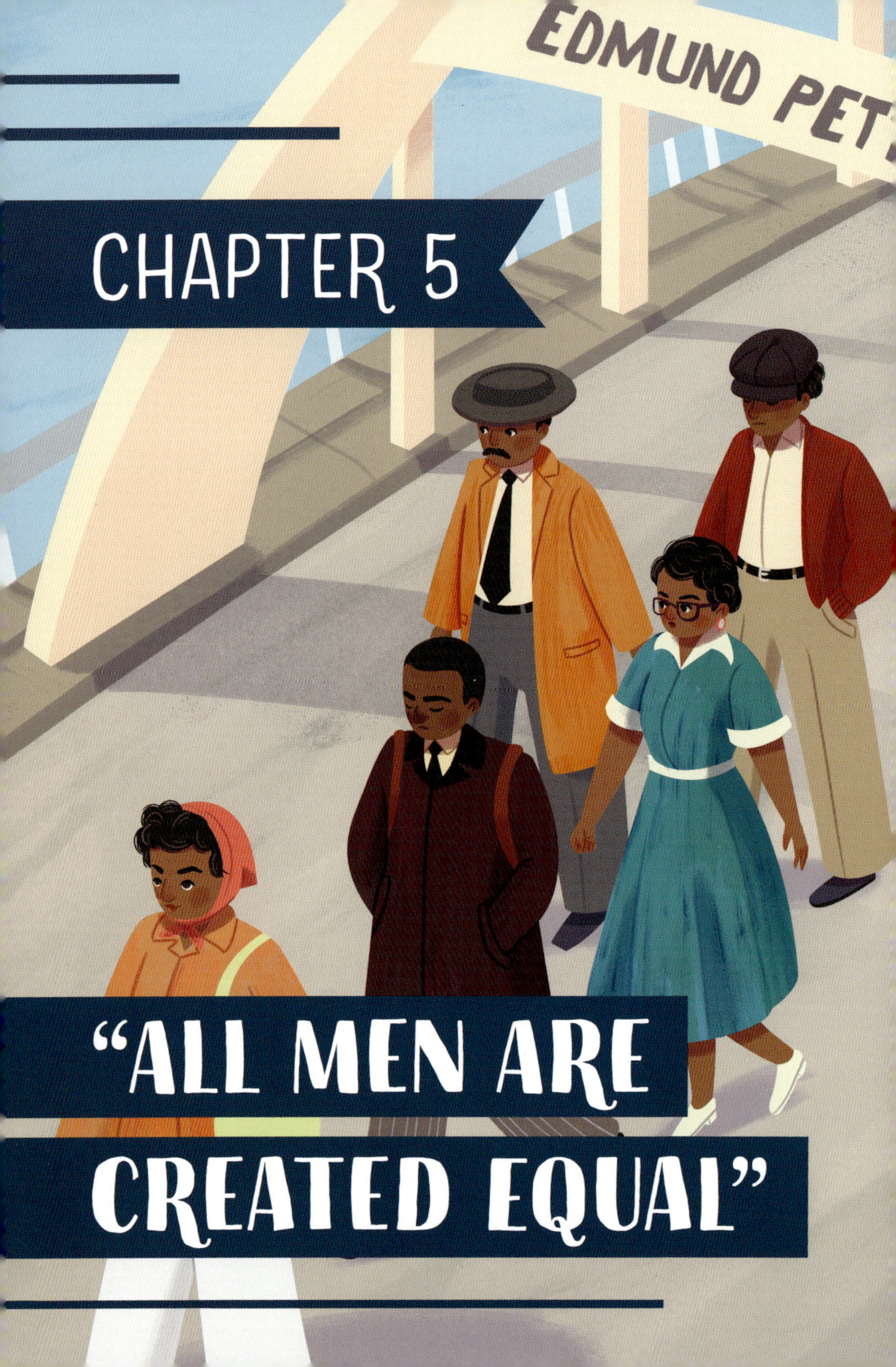

CHAPTER 5

"ALL MEN ARE CREATED EQUAL"

★ The Right to Vote ★

When the 14th Amendment was passed in 1868, it gave Black men the right to vote in elections. Southern states did not like this. They purposely made voting hard for Black men. In the South, Black people were taxed unfairly, forced to take tests, bullied, and attacked by white people who did not want them to vote. Dr. King and the SCLC stepped in to help Black people take part in elections.

There were a lot of towns in Alabama where Black people could not vote. In 1965, the SCLC and Dr. King decided to go to a bunch of those towns and protest. They would march from Selma to Montgomery, Alabama. This was called the Selma voting rights campaign.

Montgomery is the capital of Alabama. The march from Selma to Montgomery was 54 miles. As they marched, protestors were attacked and

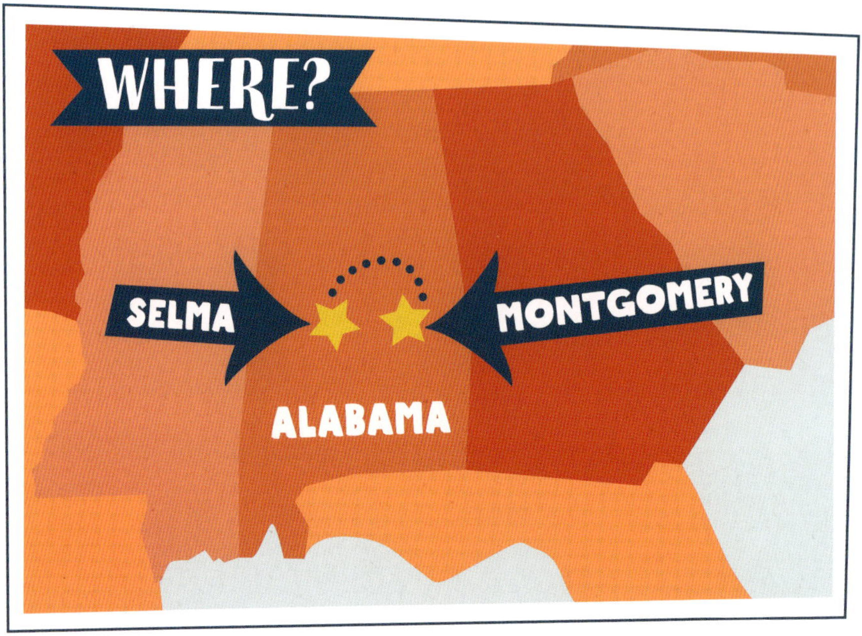

chased out of towns. President Johnson sent the US Army to protect them. When the protestors finally reached Montgomery, they were greeted by nearly 50,000 people! Black and white supporters came from all over to welcome them and Dr. King to the city.

President Johnson was very supportive of the civil rights movement and the protestors. After the Selma to Montgomery march, President Johnson asked Congress to pass a law to protect voter rights. Finally, Congress agreed to pass the Voting Rights Act of 1965. This law promised the right to vote to all Black Americans.

WHO?

Lyndon B. Johnson was the 36th president of the United States from 1963 to 1969. He signed many laws to help Black Americans, including the Civil Rights Act.

★ The Chicago Freedom Movement ★

The Civil Rights Act was passed in 1964, but there were still places where it was not followed—even in the North. The North didn't have many segregation laws, but Black people were still treated unkindly. Black people faced

JUMP –IN THE– THINK TANK

Imagine you saw someone being excluded from the rest of a group. What could you do to help them feel welcome?

discrimination at work, at school, in doctors' offices, and even in their own neighborhoods.

Even though there were no segregation laws in Chicago, many white people did anything they could to stop Black people from moving into their neighborhoods. The jobs Black people were allowed to do did not pay enough for them to buy houses. Many Black families needed to take out loans, or borrow money, to buy a house. The Federal Housing Administration was created to loan people money so they could buy houses, but it refused to give Black people loans for homes in certain neighborhoods. This meant that many Black people could only afford to live in the less desirable parts of towns.

In 1966, Dr. King and the SCLC teamed up with the Coordinating Council of Community Organizations (CCCO) to help people in Chicago peacefully protest for fair housing. Dr. King ran marches and boycotts throughout the city. Even though they were often treated poorly, the protestors stayed strong. Thousands protested in the Chicago Freedom Movement for almost two years!

Thanks to their work, the Fair Housing Act was passed in 1968. It made sure that anyone who wanted to buy a house could not be turned away based on their race, sex, or religion. This was a big step, but there was still more work to be done for all people to be treated equally.

WHEN?

MARCH 1965
Protestors march from Selma to Montgomery.

AUGUST 1965
Congress passes the Voting Rights Act.

1966
The Chicago Freedom Movement begins.

APRIL 1968
Congress passes the Fair Housing Act.

CHAPTER 6

MORE WORK TO DO

Across the Country

Black Americans were fighting for equality all over the United States. While the Chicago Freedom Movement was happening in the Midwest, people were also protesting on the West Coast. California saw many movements to support civil rights.

Black neighborhoods in Los Angeles were being treated unfairly. One of them was the Watts neighborhood. Los Angeles was an expensive city to live in. Many Black people lived in Watts because they could not afford to live anywhere else. The neighborhood was far away from nice schools and better-paying jobs. The police often patrolled the area and made unfair arrests.

Black people became very angry about how the police were treating them. In 1965, the residents of the Watts neighborhood started a riot. They inspired other Black neighborhoods across the country to stand up for themselves.

In 1966, the Black Panther Party (BPP) was created to protect the Black community. Inspired by Malcom X, Huey P. Newton and

Bobby Seale founded the BPP in Oakland, California. The BPP patrolled Black neighborhoods to make sure people were not being attacked by police officers. Later, the BPP gave food, clothing, transportation, and other important needs to Black people.

The BPP had many of the same views as Dr. Martin Luther King, Jr., but its members were also very different. Dr. King always wanted protests to be peaceful. The BPP believed in getting its point across using "any means necessary." That sometimes meant violence. The BPP grew throughout the late 1960s. It had over 2,000 members in several cities!

WHO?

Huey P. Newton helped form the Black Panther Party. He was a Black civil rights activist who helped provide important items for the Oakland community.

★ Love v. Hate ★

Can you imagine what it would be like to be arrested just for getting married? That is what happened to Mildred and Richard Loving in 1958. Mildred Loving was a Black woman, and her husband, Richard, was a white man. Virginia had a law saying that white people and Black people could not marry each other. The state of Virginia wanted to send them to prison for a year for breaking the law.

JUMP –IN THE– THINK TANK

Imagine you were arrested for loving someone. How would you feel? How do you think the Lovings felt when they won their case?

When they found out they were going to prison, they tried to **appeal** the decision. The courts in Virginia would not change their minds.

In 1967, the Supreme Court agreed to hear Mr. and Mrs. Loving's case. It is now known as *Loving v. Virginia*. All nine Supreme Court Justices agreed that it was unconstitutional for Virginia to prevent **interracial** marriage.

Everyone should have the right to eat at any restaurant, drink at any fountain, and love whomever they want—no matter their race! The people fighting for these rights believed these things so strongly that they risked their safety every day. Some people even died for their beliefs.

Dr. Martin Luther King, Jr. traveled throughout the South to help Black people gain equality. In April 1968, Dr. King went to Memphis, Tennessee, to inspire the protestors marching to support Black workers. While he was staying at the Lorraine Motel, Dr. King was shot on his balcony. He was rushed to the hospital but, sadly, passed away.

Dr. King's death marked the end of an era. The time period called the civil rights movement was over. But the work isn't finished. Until all men and women are treated equally, the fight goes on, even today.

WHEN?

- **1965**: The Watts riots occur in Los Angeles.
- **OCTOBER 1966**: Huey P. Newton and Bobby Seale start the Black Panther Party.
- **1967**: *Loving v. Virginia* makes interracial marriage legal.
- **APRIL 4 1968**: Dr. King is murdered in Memphis.

CHAPTER 7

THE MOVEMENT GOES ON

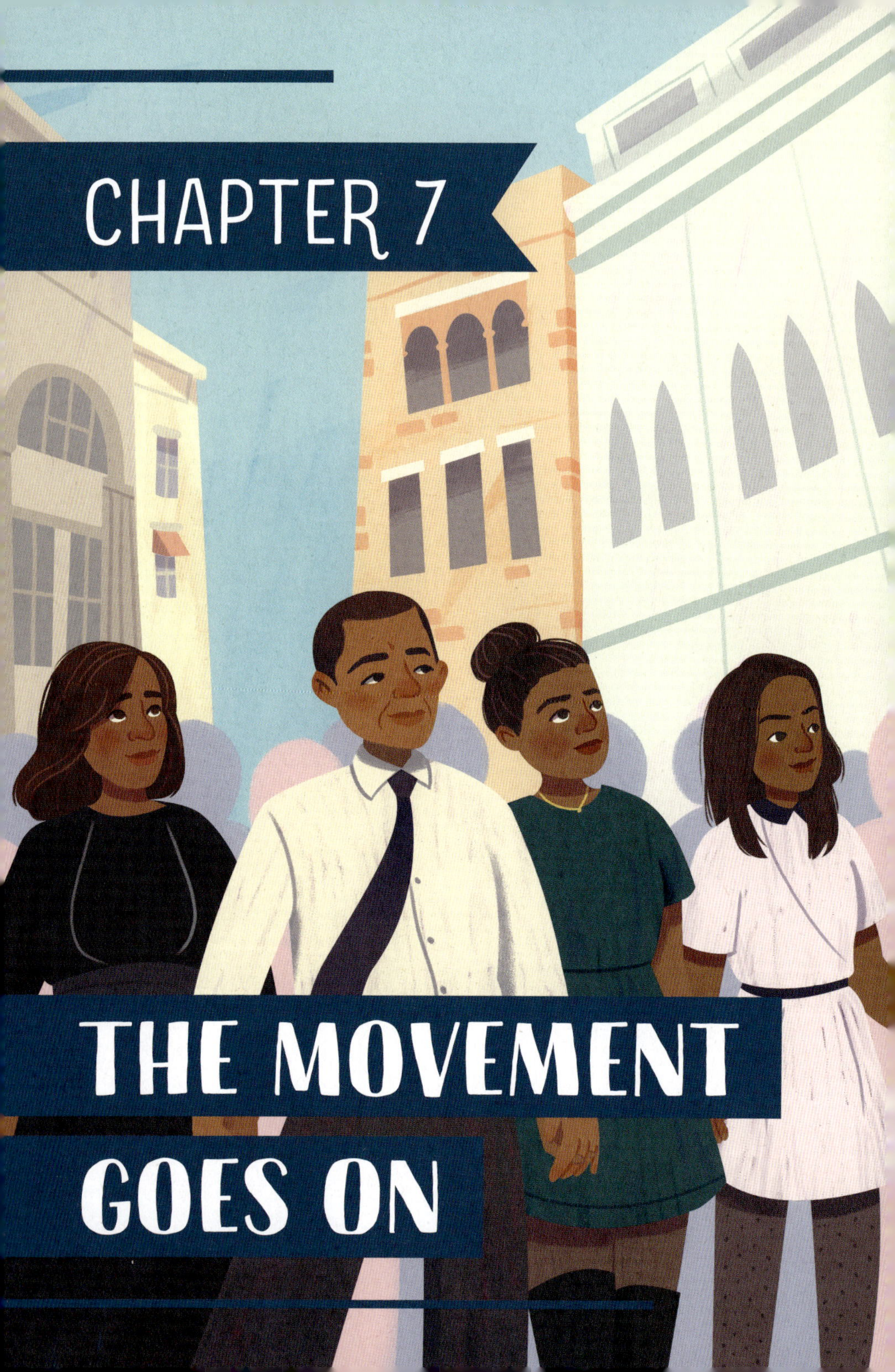

★ Civil Rights Today ★

So, what has happened since the civil rights movement ended? Many people continued to ask for equality at their jobs, in their schools, and in the public. Congress passed new laws, and Black Americans gained more equality each year. One big victory came when Congress passed the Civil Rights Act of 1991. It said that companies couldn't use color, gender, religion, or **ethnicity** to reject a person for a job.

The fight for equal rights stretched into the 1990s. When unfair things happened, people asked why. Those people were not afraid to stand up for fairness and justice. Today, there are still many groups and people who promote civil rights. There are rallies, protests, marches, and boycotts just like there were in the 1960s.

The United States has changed for the better since the time of Dr. King and Rosa Parks.

In 2008, America had a very big change. A Black senator from Illinois became president of the United States. Barack Obama led the way for many Black Americans in politics.

While Obama was president, civil rights got a lot of attention. Schools created new volunteer programs to help kids succeed and get good grades. More **minority** students graduated from high school than the years before.

JUMP IN THE THINK TANK

What are some small things you can do today to fight for equality?

WHO?

Stacey Abrams is a lawyer and politician from Georgia. She is also an activist and an author!

President Obama's time in office also encouraged other Black people to enter politics. Stacey Abrams is one Black woman who made history. She served in the Georgia House of Representatives for 11 years. Then, in 2018, Stacey became the first Black woman to run for governor of Georgia.

★ A Better Tomorrow ★

It's true that the United States has come far in civil rights. However, there is still more to do. Sadly, Black people and other minorities still face **prejudice** and **racism** today.

One of the biggest problems is the way police officers treat people of color. There have been many cases in the United States where police officers have pulled Black people over while they were driving—without any good reason. Over the years, many Black people have also been unfairly killed by the police.

In 2012, a high school student named Trayvon Martin was murdered in Sanford, Florida, on his way back from a store. Someone who lived in the neighborhood thought Trayvon looked

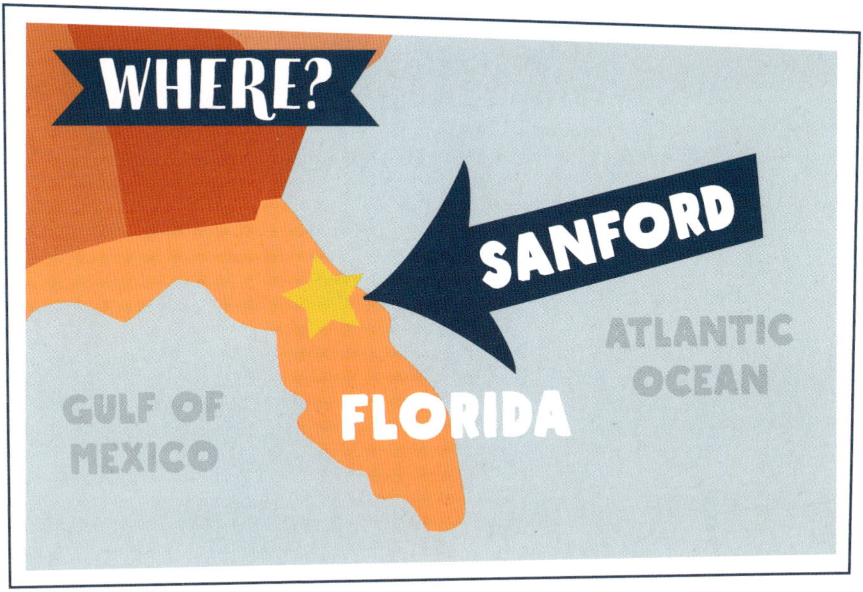

dangerous and shot him. Just because someone looks different doesn't mean they are dangerous.

People all over the country were upset by Trayvon's death. As a result, three brave women—Alicia Garza, Patrisse Cullors, and Opal Tometi—started the Black Lives Matter (BLM) movement. They wanted to remind people that Black people and their lives are important. BLM fought and continues to fight for the fair treatment of Black people by the police.

In recent years, the Black Lives Matter movement has done many great things for Black Americans. BLM has inspired companies and businesses to make sure all of their employees are treated fairly and equally. Their work has also helped change the way police officers are trained. Sadly, there have been other Black people since Trayvon who have been wrongfully killed. Black Lives Matter continues to bring attention to the work left to do. Every day, there is an opportunity to make a difference. What will you do to make a better tomorrow?

WHEN?

1991
Civil Rights Act of 1991 is passed.

2009
Barack Obama becomes the first Black president of the United States.

2012
Trayvon Martin is killed, and Black Lives Matter is founded.

CHAPTER 8

SO . . . WHAT'S THE HISTORY OF THE CIVIL RIGHTS MOVEMENT ?

★ Challenge Accepted! ★

You've read the book, so now let's put your knowledge of the civil rights movement to the test! The answers follow, but don't peek!

1 **What issue started the Civil War?**

→ A. Slavery
→ B. Taxes
→ C. Artwork
→ D. Money

2 **When was the civil rights movement?**

→ A. 1920s–1930s
→ B. 1950s–1960s
→ C. 1940s–1950s
→ D. 1980s–1990s

3 **What was *Brown v. Board of Education* about?**

→ A. Free school lunch

→ B. Longer recess time

→ C. Desegregating schools

→ D. School bus transportation

4 **Where was Dr. King's famous bus boycott?**

→ A. Washington, DC

→ B. Iuka, Mississippi

→ C. Atlanta, Georgia

→ D. Montgomery, Alabama

5 **Who was the first Black student to go to William Frantz Elementary School?**

→ A. Rosa Parks

→ B. Malcom X

→ C. Ruby Bridges

→ D. Oliver Brown

6 **Who was Thurgood Marshall?**

- A. A lawyer
- B. A doctor
- C. An activist
- D. A politician

7 **Who asked Congress to pass the Voting Rights Act of 1965?**

- A. John F. Kennedy
- B. Richard Nixon
- C. Lyndon B. Johnson
- D. Abraham Lincoln

8 **Where did the Children's Crusade take place?**

- A. Selma, Alabama
- B. Los Angeles, California
- C. Chicago, Illinois
- D. Birmingham, Alabama

9 What was *Plessy v. Ferguson*?

→ A. The Supreme Court ruling that made segregation legal

→ B. A famous boxing match

→ C. The band that played at the March on Washington

→ D. The case that made biracial marriage legal

10 Black Lives Matter started as . . .

→ A. A news story

→ B. A civil rights band

→ C. A fight for equal education

→ D. A protest against the unfair treatment of Black people by the police

Answers: 1. A, 2. B, 3. C, 4. D, 5. C, 6. A, 7. C, 8. D, 9. A, 10. D

★ Our World ★

The civil rights movement changed the United States for the better. The movement started a fight for equality that is still happening today!

→ The American Association of University Women (AAUW) fights for equal pay for Black women—and all women. Most recently, it helped support the Paycheck Fairness Act. The act will help make sure employees get equal pay no matter their race or gender.

→ Kamala Harris made history in 2021 as the first woman and the first Black American to serve as the vice president of the United States. She is dedicated to civil rights. Kamala has fought to improve how the police force interacts with the public in California. She also works to support children's rights.

→ The American Civil Liberties Union (ACLU) is an important organization that continues to fight for equality. It helps take cases to the Supreme Court. The ACLU also hosts marches and rallies.

JUMP IN THE THINK TANK FOR MORE!

No one is too young to think about how they can support the fight for civil rights. Read these questions and think about ways you can make a difference!

→ Think about your friends and family. How has the civil rights movement impacted you?

→ Dr. King and other civil rights leaders did everything they could to educate people. What are some ways you can teach others about the civil rights movement?

→ Black Americans spent many years left out of society. What are some ways you can make sure everyone feels included?

→ Can you think of something you'd like to try to change when you are older? You may make history one day!

Glossary

activist: A person who works to bring about change for something they care very much about

appeal: To ask a higher court to review the decision of a lower court

boycott: To stop buying something or using a service as a form of protest

civil rights: Basic rights that every person has under the laws of the government to be treated fairly and equally

colonist: A person who has settled in a new place

Constitution of the United States: A document written in 1787 after the United States became a country that states basic laws and rules for how the country should be run

desegregate: To end laws, policies, or both that keep races apart

discrimination: The unfair treatment of a person or group of people, based on where they come from, what they look like, what religion they are, or if they are men or women

enslaved people: People forced into slavery

equality: When every person has the same rights and opportunities

ethnicity: The culture of a group of people that includes their customs, language, and traditions

federal marshal: A high-ranking law officer who works for the government of the United States

Freedom Rides: A form of protest in the 1960s where Black Americans rode public buses through the segregated South

interracial: Involving members of different races

Interstate Commerce Commission: The government organization that controlled buses, trains, boats, and other transportation between states

Jim Crow laws: Laws allowing the segregation of Black Americans

minority: A group that is different in some way from the larger group

movement: When a group of people gets together to change the rules set up by the government

National Association for the Advancement of Colored People (NAACP): An organization that fights to end segregation in voting, education, housing, and other areas

National Guard: A group of the American military

national origin: The nation or country where someone is born

prejudice: Having an opinion about someone based on how they look, where they come from, or what religion they practice

protestor: Someone who disagrees with something and speaks out about it

racism: Discrimination against someone of a different race based on the belief that one's own race is better

segregate: To separate people, usually based on their race or skin color

sit-in: A type of peaceful protest where people refuse to leave a space

slavery: A system in which people are treated like property and forced to work against their will for no pay

Supreme Court: The highest court in the United States

unconstitutional: Going against the rights granted by the US Constitution

Bibliography

Azhary, ElMehdi El. "The Children's Crusade of Birmingham." Medium. January 19, 2021. Medium.com/lessons-from-history/the-childrens-crusade-of-birmingham-b3cd8c115d17.

Ducksters. "American Civil War." Accessed June 2, 2021. Ducksters.com/history/civil_war/causes_of_the_civil_war.php.

History. "Loving v. Virginia." Last modified January 25, 2021. History.com/topics/civil-rights-movement/loving-v-virginia.

Join Stacey Abrams. "Stacey Abrams for Governor." Accessed June 28, 2021. StaceyAbrams.com.

Smith, Doug. "Stunned by the Watts Riots, the L.A. Times Struggled to Make Sense of the Violence." *The Los Angeles Times.* August 12, 2015. Graphics.LATimes.com/watts-annotations.

The US National Archives and Records Administration. "The Black Panther Party." Last modified March 22, 2021. Archives.gov/research/african-americans/black-power/black-panthers.

The White House President Barack Obama. "Strengthening Civil Rights." Accessed May 25, 2021. ObamaWhiteHouse.Archives.gov/issues/civil-rights.

About the Author

Shadae Mallory is a writer, educator, and social justice advocate. They received their master of arts in higher education from Bowling Green State University and their bachelor of arts in English from the University of Northern Colorado. Shadae also works as a diversity, equity, and inclusion consultant and as a freelance writer. *The History of the Civil Rights Movement* is Shadae's first book. You can follow Shadae online at ShadaeMallory.com.

About the Illustrator

Angie Alape was born in Colombia. She grew up drawing on every cardboard box around her, making all kinds of nonexistent worlds in which to play with her siblings. She has been working as a freelance illustrator since her first collaboration with a Chilean editorial. Alape has worked in editorial publishing, social campaigns, character design for 3D animation, and web magazines. In her spare time, you can find her playing with her adopted dogs and looking for places to enjoy a nice weekend meal.

WHO WILL INSPIRE YOU NEXT?

EXPLORE A WORLD OF HEROES AND ROLE MODELS IN ***THE STORY OF...*** BIOGRAPHY SERIES FOR NEW READERS.

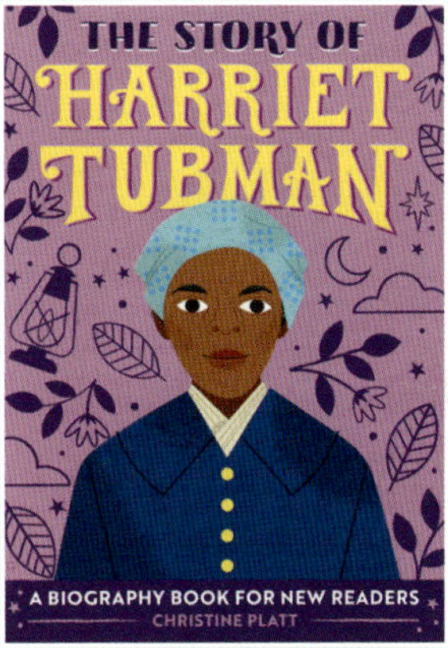

LOOK FOR THIS SERIES
WHEREVER BOOKS AND EBOOKS ARE SOLD

Ruby Bridges
Albert Einstein
Martin Luther King Jr.
George Washington
Jane Goodall
Barack Obama
Helen Keller
Marie Curie